Mind Games

25 Thought Experiments to Ignite Your Imagination

Todd William

Published in the United States by Zaze & Drury Publishing House.
ISBN: 978-0692604793

This book is presented to you for entertainment purposes only and is not a substitution for any professional advice or opinion. The contents herein are based on the views and opinions of the author and all associated contributors.

While every effort has been made by the author and all associated contributors to present accurate and up to date information within this document, it is apparent technologies rapidly change. Therefore, the author and all associated contributors reserve the right to update the contents and information provided herein as these changes progress. The author and/or all associated contributors take no responsibility for any errors or omissions if such discrepancies exist within this document.

CONTENTS

THOUGHT EXPERIMENT
/ NOUN /

- **A QUESTION OR SCENARIO THAT EXPLORES THE CONSEQUENCES OF AN IDEA**
- **AN EXERCISE USED TO IMAGINE THE PRACTICAL OUTCOME OF A HYPOTHESIS**
- **A MIND-BLOWINGLY BRILLIANT WAY TO GIVE YOUR BRAIN A WORKOUT**

Introduction

Our imagination knows no bounds. There is no single thought we cannot envision other than that which has not occurred to us. It is limitless.

Within our minds, we can travel to distant places inaccessible by our bodies. We can produce ideas, consider extremes, contemplate things that never were, and conceptualize a future that has not yet occurred.

Imagination is to the mind as air to our lungs - an essential element of life. What we do with our imagination is what matters most.

The Thought Experiment

One of the finest expressions of imagination is the thought experiment: a device used to investigate the nature of things. Conducted entirely in our minds, it is not constrained by resources, technological capabilities, finances, or even ethics. This kind of experimentation is not even bound by reality.

Thought experiments have been a mainstay of deep thinkers for thousands of years. Many of history's greatest minds have used them, ranging from **Zeno's** arrow, **Galileo's** falling objects, **Einstein's** beam of light, to **Schrödinger's** Cat. Posing questions in this manner has helped mankind to explore theories, explain concepts and engage imaginations for the entirety of recorded history.

Good thought experiments stretch your mind, providing a mental workout; something that should be of interest to anyone who values intellectual health. Yet there are many more ways to benefit from conducting thought experiments.

Entertainment

One of the most exciting features of thought experimentation is the propensity to introduce mind-blowing ideas. Anyone who enjoyed ***The Matrix*** can relate.

The movie is based on the famous **Brain in a Vat** thought experiment. You are asked to imagine the possibility that you are a brain hooked up to a sophisticated computer capable of providing electrical impulses that perfectly simulate reality. If true, there would be no rational way to know that you are being deceived - and there you have one of the most intriguing movie twists of all time.

Humility

Thought experiments often provide insights that will influence the way you think for the rest of your life. One such example is **Plato's Cave** - which asks you to imagine three prisoners who have been chained in a cave their entire lives.

Having only faced the cave wall, their entire knowledge of the outside world is the shadows of activity that appear on the surface of the rock. The result is that they are led to believe the shadows are not mere reflections, but are reality itself.

One of the prisoners escapes and is shocked to discover that his former view of reality was severely lacking. He returns to the cave to find that he's unable to convey this knowledge to the other prisoners as they lack the context to understand. They refuse to acknowledge the possibility that there is more to life than what they know.

Given the volume of beliefs we all hold, based on our personal perceptions of reality, it is impossible to absorb the message in this thought experiment without gaining an improved sense of humility.

Ingenuity

Thought experiments are a great source of ingenuity because they cater to the curious. Every great invention first had to begin with someone asking, "**what if**..."

- **What if** we put a circle on the side of a cart?
- **What if** we could harness the power of electricity?
- **What if** we found a way to get Internet access on our phones?

Someone out there, right now, is probably contemplating an idea that will lead to a revolutionary new concept. These ideas begin as thoughts, and examining them in your head is how you bring them to fruition. Thought experiments are the workplace of the imagination, and one of the best methods to have a constant stream of ideas popping into your mind.

Comprehension

Sometimes, the best way to illustrate a complicated concept is by using a story or situation.

For most people, the notion that the curvature of space is responsible for gravitational effects, rather than a pulling force, is very difficult to grasp. Yet when you consider a bowling ball sitting in the middle of a trampoline, and imagine rolling a marble from the edge, it's easy to see how a large object causing a curve in a medium (in this case the trampoline) can directly affect the path of other objects without actually interacting with them.

Just as with sports, once you learn the fundamentals, you can reach higher levels of competence. The accumulation of knowledge often operates the same, because grasping a difficult yet fundamental concept opens the doors to deeper levels of understanding.

Wisdom

Thought Experiments have been helping you since you were a child. ***The Tortoise and the Hare*** poses a scenario that helped you understand patience. ***The Three Little Pigs*** taught you that being lazy can be costly. And the story of ***The Emperor's New Clothes*** demonstrates the ridiculousness of blindly agreeing with popular opinion. When you think about it, you have used and valued thought experiments your whole life.

Ethics

Thought experiments help you to better contemplate difficult ethical questions.

The Trolley Problem is a thought experiment that presents a scenario with a runaway trolley on course to knock over five people. You have the ability to divert the trolley to a different track, but doing so will cause it to run over a single person who otherwise wouldn't have been harmed. What do you do?

There are no easy answers here, but thinking about these types of scenarios helps you to build a moral framework that will aide you in decision making throughout your whole life.

Purpose of this Book

Mind Games is a collection of 25 thought experiments. Each chapter represents an individual experiment, permitting you to begin at any point in the book and skip around if you desire.

Among them you will find topics ranging from science, mathematics, morality, social issues, to the very essence of our own minds. It is my great hope that contemplating these experiments will entertain your curiosity while simultaneously igniting your imagination.

Though our collective level of knowledge may always be defined by a certain set of answers, we are never limited by the questions we may pose, and this is where the fun begins.

Enjoy.

1 ~ The Origin of the Universe

When a ball is thrown vertically into the air, it decelerates until it reaches a peak, stops, and then begins to accelerate back to the ground. You have the earth's gravitational pull to thank for this.

If you look at a short interval that spans the period of time when the ball is going up and recognize that it is decelerating, you can calculate how high the ball will go, and how long it will take to reach its peak. This is simple physics.

However, if you look only at a short interval that spans when the ball is going back down, and recognize it is accelerating toward the ground, it is not clear where the ball began. Using the same laws of physics, you can calculate backwards to the point when the ball began its downward movement, but nothing before that. You can even calculate the amount of time that has passed since it began accelerating (its peak).

But this says nothing of its actual beginning, which

took place long before this point in time. Without knowing how the ball initially got to the point at its peak, no amount of calculations can tell you whether the ball was initially thrown from a different point or just dropped at a particular height. In fact, the variables would be the exact same for this snapshot in either scenario.

Now consider how we look at the universe. It has been observed that the universe is accelerating in an outward direction. Using basic mathematical formulas, we can calculate backwards to a single point in time about 13.8 billion years ago when this acceleration began. And as a result, we have assumed this is the beginning of the universe.

Yet just like the ball, there are multiple ways to account for acceleration. If we observed a ball that had been decelerating downward for 13.8 seconds, we've only determined at what point it reached its peak, not when it began. In fact, 13.8 seconds ago, it would have only reached the halfway point along its journey.

When viewing only intervals where the universe is accelerating, there is no reason to presume we know how it reached this point. Would there be any reason to assume that the ball must have begun its motion with a bang?

What if it was the Opposite?

Imagine the universe as a giant sphere, only with a gravitational pull outwards, rather than a push from a big bang. If all matter was "thrown" inward, it would gradually decelerate, stop, and begin accelerating outward, just as we observe the universe today.

Perhaps something far bigger than we have imagined and beyond what we can observe is pulling us outward.

What if the universe didn't begin 13.8 billion years ago and, just like the ball, the acceleration we are observing is a sign that it is returning to its true origin?

2 ~ Social Norms

Take a brief look through history and you'll soon discover that many disturbing ideas often represented the prevailing views of society. How could anyone have defended things like slavery, witch trials, or the burning of heretics?

Yet these ideas weren't exclusive to fools or the morally depraved. Many people we consider highly intelligent are often found on the wrong side of morality in a number of these areas.

Aristotle held the belief that women should be subservient to men. More recent history shows that a number of the US Founding Fathers not only supported the idea of slavery, but had slaves of their own.

Most would argue these are horrible views. So how could this be? How could intelligent people have been so blatantly misguided?

All these issues were hotly debated at some point in history. You can actually read the transcripts of the deliberations on issues like slavery and women's rights where the intellectuals of the time were closely split.

It was only well after one side prevailed that it seemed so atrocious to have been on the wrong side of the debate.

It's easy to look back now that these issues are settled, but are you really so morally superior to those from the past? Or is it possible that on some issues, you benefit from society having already established its moral position?

Consider for a moment if you've ever had to seriously weigh in your mind the fairness of slave ownership. This is an issue that has been settled in Western society your entire lifetime.

You're not burdened with having to debate the morality of this in society nor in your own mind. But if you were born in 1800, you were just as likely to grow up leaning the opposite direction merely based on where and when you were born.

You may tell yourself that you'd view some issues the same no matter what, but are you really so sure? Are you certain you'd be one of the few to stand up for what is morally right, even if the entirety of society disagreed?

Societal Influence

Most people grossly underestimate the influence that society has on their thinking. It is human nature to accept ready-made opinions as your own without really giving them much thought, and then justify these views by regurgitating well known rationalizations.

Take the idea of buying a diamond engagement ring. The term "blood diamond" exists because too many of the diamonds we treasure are brought to us in exchange for the death and suffering of millions of people. The diamond mining industry reveals a history of horrible exploitation of third world nations. Even though it is now possible to efficiently produce man-made diamonds indistinguishable to the naked eye from real diamonds, society still deems wearing one of these to be in poor taste.

It's no great leap to think that future historians might look back with disgust at the notion that so many of us valued these stones more than the dignity and lives of millions of people, and all for very superficial reasons.

But this isn't about diamonds, it is about social norms. Are you really so certain you're on the right side of every issue, or might some of your views be the result of when you were born rather than genuine morality?

3 ~ Infinity

If you take 5 numbered blocks and arrange them in a straight line, there are only 120 possible arrangements you can build. Suppose you place them in a particular arrangement.

After being mixed up and placed in another line in random order, the probability of having the original arrangement of blocks reoccur is therefore 1/120, which is roughly 0.8%.

However, the more often the blocks are randomly placed in a line, the greater chances that the original line will appear. If you've taken any basic probability course (assuming you passed), this should be fairly obvious. But let's look at the breakdown.

- **At 5 iterations the probability is about 4%**
- **At 50 iterations the probability is about 34%**
- **At 500 iterations the probability is about 98%**
- **At 5000 iterations the probability is effectively 1**

(The MATH: $P = 1-(119/120)^N$ where N is the number of iterations).

It should be no surprise that, with increased volume, the likelihood of unlikely events goes up tremendously. This is why lotteries with millions of possible number combinations are won on a regular basis.

The underlying message here is this: with any finite set of possibilities, the probability of this set reoccurring randomly always approaches 1 with every additional iteration.

Here is where things get interesting. If you have an infinite number of iterations, the expectation of any recurrence not only reaches 1, but the probability of an infinite number of recurrences also equals 1.

To put that in layman's terms, if you take the 5 blocks in a line and randomly put them into new lines an infinite number of times, mathematically speaking, you will not only expect to see that original pattern reemerge, you will expect it to reemerge an infinite number of times.

When thinking in terms of the blocks, that may seem painfully obvious. But in large numbers, it becomes very counter intuitive.

Consider the fixed number of atoms in our Solar System. They can conceivably be formulated in a mind-boggling number of different arrangements. Yet however large the number, it is still finite.

But we Don't Know that the Universe is Finite.

As many hypothesize, the universe may in fact be infinite. We may never know for sure, but two things we can state with certainty are:

- **There are a finite number of atoms in our solar system.**

- **There are a finite number of combinations that these atoms can be arranged into, one of which is our solar system.**

We can therefore conclude that with an infinite universe that contains an infinite number of arrangements of atoms, the probability of an identical solar system, complete with a duplicate earth and another physical version of you and everyone you know is equal to 1 ~ effectively guaranteed.

4 ~ The Island

If you found yourself on a deserted island, with no hope of being found, what might your top priorities be? If you chose to live, it would no doubt be **water** and **food**, followed by some sort of **shelter**.

Once you've established these, ensuring your **safety** and **health** would soon follow. And should those needs be met, you could then get to work improving the quality of your life.

The less time you have to waste gathering food, repairing your shelter, or running from danger, the more time you have to spend doing whatever you would like to do.

Reality

But this is considerably different from ordinary life. For one, we have different objectives. We don't merely eat food to live, we live to eat good foods. We don't just care about shelter, we care about curb appeal.

Our everyday needs are so easily met that almost all of our focus and concerns are directed toward things that are not essential to life, they are just creature comforts. We are very fortunate to live in a time when we can concern ourselves mostly with how we want to improve our lives, not merely with maintaining life.

We have no reason to apologize for this. We don't live on a deserted island, and improving our quality of life has value. That we've reached a point where most of our daily efforts are put towards creature comforts, rather than necessities, is a fine tribute to human ingenuity. Yet the implications of this are easily overlooked.

Jobs

Most jobs are not about necessities, they are about creature comforts - the icing on the cake. Once you move beyond things that involve food, water, housing, safety, and health, the necessity of any job begins to quickly fall into the that grey area where usefulness is purely subjective.

The point isn't that these jobs aren't worthwhile, it's that we're addicted to the icing, and we should be. Why not improve our lives? But this addiction keeps us blind to the possibilities.

Technology

We've reached a point where we can realistically discuss the possibility of a future when technology is able to replace most jobs. It's a scary notion. Yet maybe it shouldn't be.

If the use of technology permits us to produce all of

life's essentials with negligible manual effort, then all jobs would be related to icing (the "non-essentials"). Any job losses related to technology would merely determine the amount of icing any of us would share.

There would no doubt be disparity, but in exchange, the notion of working to "get by" would be gone. Life would suddenly be merely a matter of how you decide to use your time - and that has more to do with imagination than circumstance.

This is a hard concept to fathom because we're so accustomed to assessing the value of our lives by comparing what we possess relative to those around us.

But isn't it more appealing to judge the value of life by the amount of quality time we have at our disposal? That is the great equalizer. No matter how much power, wealth, or influence you have, you're still getting the same 24 hours a day that we all get.

The Island

We don't live on an isolated island, but we do live on an isolated planet. Maybe it's not so different after all, we just need to get over our addiction to the non-essentials.

Consider for a moment what it would mean if you no longer felt compelled to always have more. If food, water, shelter, health, and safety was all guaranteed to you, might you look at your job differently?

Would you feel a bit more selective on how you use your time?

5 ~ The Evolution of Recording

Think for a moment about the process that humans have used to record events throughout history.

The first evidence we know of is paintings on cave walls. A little further along in time, after many intermediate steps, we see the development of writing. In the more recent past, we see the invention of the camera, audio recording devices, and ultimately video.

The manner in which humans have recorded history (and to a lesser extent our own lives) has evolved. We've come a long way.

Consider the implications of time. Much of the technology we take for granted today was pure **science fiction** 50-100 years ago, **a dream** 200 years ago, and **inconceivable** 500 years ago. Using these groupings of viewpoints, we can project into the future and categorize the possibilities.

In the Realm of Science Fiction...

The use of holograms has been well done in science fiction – most notably Star Wars and Star Trek. We're already seeing the beginnings of this technology – a moon-walking Michael Jackson hologram performing on stage with live dancers. It's no real stretch to imagine recorded video in a holographic form.

Recent breakthroughs in cognitive neuroscience have produced devices capable of recording thoughts. These are very crude mechanisms well short of anything commercially practical. Yet most inventions are at the outset. Consider the first sound recordings by Edison or the first aerial flights by the Wright brothers. Both represented very primitive models of today's complex versions. What is important to understand is that the science to record thoughts is here, and the possibilities are intriguing. What would it mean to record your thoughts, dreams, or even memories?

Is it too unimaginable to think that recording devices of this nature might appear in the next 50-100 years?

In the Realm of Dreams...

Whatever the future of recording will be, it will need to be based on the sensory inputs we currently use to perceive our reality. If not, there would be no value in playback.

What then, are we left with when we've maxed out our imaginations on sight and sounds? Smell? That's too boring.

What if you could record your emotions and relive moments of your past based on how they made you feel instead of just watching and listening? What if you could submerge yourself in a virtual reality playback that reproduced your neural activity from a prior experience providing the exact same sensations of touch?

Before your mind hits the gutter, consider the implications of recording devices that could reproduce moments based on emotion and touch. We have no basis for how this could be done, but science is beginning to understand emotional states and chemical imbalances. We also know a bit about nerve endings, so we know where to look. Is it too much of a leap to think we might have some breakthroughs in this area in the next 200 years?

In the Realm of Inconceivability…

What if you could record your entire life, and live it back exactly as it was within your last moments. Or even better, what if you could play it on an infinite loop outside the realm of time?

Inconceivable? I hope you're at least thinking that a little, because if not, I'm clearly not very imaginative. None of us can possibly know the extent of how far humans will push technology. It's all conjecture.

But if you read this far and think all this speculation seems too far-fetched, consider one thing: If you feel the manner in which humans record life isn't likely to continue evolving, then you're left having to accept that the recording technology of today represents the peak of human ingenuity. Does that seem less far-fetched?

6 ~ Emergence

Of the 26 letters in the English alphabet, none imply anything complex. They represent a sound or character. Yet arrange them with other letters to form words and meaning emerges. Take these words and form sentences, then paragraphs, and ultimately you can produce content that inspires emotion, passion, and inspiration. That writing can produce feelings in others is a profound concept.

Emergent Properties

By taking single elements that lack any deep meaning on their own, and organizing them into complex arrangements, you can express deep qualities that are not easy to construct. This is the essence of emergent properties.

Somewhere along the spectrum that ranges from individual letters to written content, you transition from mere symbols to profound meaning – but where? This is not so easy to answer.

While it's silly to look for profound qualities in a single letter, it is quite common to recognize them in writing. It's easy to accept this leap without any need for mystical or supernatural explanations.

Atoms

We are all made of atoms. Everything in the known universe is made up atoms. Arrange them into certain forms and you have a molecule, something much more meaningful.

With enough of the appropriate molecules you have biological matter and, ultimately, with all the right combinations, life emerges: matter becomes self-aware. Quite a leap.

It would be just as ridiculous to look for self-awareness in a single atom as it would be to search for such qualities as inspiration in a single letter.

By following the same reasoning, self-awareness may be said to be an emergent property of a complex arrangement of atoms, just as inspiration is described as an emergent quality of a complex arrangement of letters.

The Spectrum

What if, along the spectrum of emergence, self-awareness is similar to words rather than writing? Words have meaning. They have qualities of much more substance than single letters. Yet despite being higher along the spectrum, words are not the pinnacle. Perhaps self-awareness is not the peak either.

We look at the spider building its web and admit that there is something remarkable about this process. Yet we attribute little more than instinct to the spider – certainly nothing close to human intelligence. We do this only because we're aware of something much greater.

Instinct is rudimentary in comparison to self-awareness. If we knew of nothing more complex than instinct, on what basis could we offer judgment?

We're not aware of something more profound than self-awareness because we've yet to observe anything to make us believe such a thing exists. What if self-awareness is a mere building block leading to something far more profound – something that, if arranged in just the right manner, would produce emergent qualities beyond the scope of our imagination?

7 ~ The Expanding Universe

Consider the night sky. Scientific consensus says that the universe is currently expanding faster than the speed of light.

The best way to conceptualize this is to imagine two points on the edge of a balloon. As the balloon expands, the distance between these points grows. In the same sense, everything in the universe, all the galaxies and stars within them, is affected by the expansion of space. The only difference is space expands in three dimensions.

What is revealed to us with our most advanced instruments is limited to the speed of light, which is what makes up the observable universe. We can only speculate what is beyond this point.

With this in mind, at some point millions of years into the future, all the galaxies that we can now detect will have expanded beyond the reach of light. We will no longer see them or be able to detect them in any way under the known laws of physics. It will be as though they no longer exist.

What happens if life on another planet in a distant galaxy develops after this period of time? Suppose they reach the same level of scientific sophistication we have now. They could have all the equivalent methods, capabilities, and scientific understanding we have yet would amass entirely different data without ever knowing that something was missing.

In fact, for this future life form, all the best data would suggest they live in a single galaxy in the midst of an infinite empty space. Simply because of time, their understanding of the universe would be severely lacking, yet perfectly credible given the circumstances.

What if we are that life form?

How do we even know what we might be missing? What information might no longer be available to us that would tell an entirely different story about the state of the universe? What if our questions about why the universe is expanding had been obvious in a prior time?

8 ~ The Illusion of Control

Our senses are easily fooled, often times in enjoyable ways. Anyone who has viewed the talents of sidewalk 3D artists will attest that illusions, when done right, are incredible.

Nature contributes her own illusions, a simple mirage perhaps being the best demonstration of such natural trickery. But nature also provides many far more compelling illusions.

The Geocentric Model

For thousands of years, the entirety of humanity believed that the sun and stars revolved around a stationary earth. This was a justified view. The earth feels stationary, and unless our eyes deceive us, we all have a lifetime of confirming evidence.

Yet our eyes do deceive us, because the geocentric model (the entire universe revolving around the earth) is a fantastic illusion. Though we may mock the notion of believing such a thing now, had we been born six centuries ago, there's no doubt we would have assumed this illusion to be truth. And who could blame us for thinking so?

In fact, if you lived in that time period and attempted to explain the fallacy of a geocentric model, you would have had one heck of a time convincing anyone, because the idea would have seemed inconceivable. That is the basis of any great illusion.

Visual Field

Though few remain tied to the notion of geocentric model, there are other known illusions that we persist in believing because we don't consider the mechanics of what is taking place.

It is natural to assume we have a continuous view in our visual fields - the stuff we are seeing in front of our face. But this isn't so either. We actually have a blind spot as there are no cells to detect light on the optic disc at the back of our retinas. We don't realize this because our brains are well equipped to fill in the void with information to give the appearance of continuity.

That we have a blind spot right in front of our faces and don't even notice is quite telling. It means we are easily fooled when we don't give much consideration to the mechanics of what is actually taking place. This is another element of a great illusion.

This leads to perhaps the most fascinating illusion of all, one that seems inconceivable and contains mechanics that are easily overlooked.

Origin of Thoughts

Ever had an idea just pop into your mind for reasons you can't explain? This is best described as a spontaneous thought - a thought that arrives in your consciousness for reasons unknown or unexplainable to you.

There are a number of possible explanations to account for spontaneous thoughts. Yet no matter what the explanation, one thing remains true: if you cannot explain nor know the origin of a thought, logically speaking, there is no way to demonstrate that you intended the thought.

But most thoughts don't seem spontaneous, they happen for a good reason. We decide to think about bicycles, and bicycle related ideas begin to flow, thus we can lay claim for originating the thought. But can we really?

Causality

This brings up a question of causality. By definition, if there is a cause that produces an effect, that effect had to have occurred unless the conditions of the cause had been different. Thus unless we originated the cause of a thought, then we can't logically make any claims to its origin...unless we somehow controlled the origin of the cause itself.

In a game of billiards, if the 8-ball begins moving because it was stuck by another ball, there is a defined cause. If we want to know why it moved, we'd merely need to know why the other ball crashed into it (the cause). Yet if the other ball began moving because it was also stuck, then we need to go back another step to find its cause, and so on.

Eventually, we'd find a cue ball that was stuck by a cue, which would seem to be the answer as to why the 8-ball ultimately moved. What is important to recognize is that there is no value in assessing the intermediate causes to answer this question, because we need to find the origin of those causes to determine the controlling factors.

But with thoughts, this is problematic. Causality is a very tricky beast. To claim responsibility for any thought that has a prior cause, we have to go back through a chain of causality until we reach a cause that had no prior cause itself - the thought that originated the entire process.

A Thought with no Cause?

Even if such a thing is possible, logically speaking, something without a cause, with respect to our consciousness, is no different than a spontaneous thought. There is no logical way to control something that has no cause, because a controlling factor would be a cause.

The alternative is to deal with issues of infinite regress, whereby each cause is merely preceded by another cause going back indefinitely. But like the billiard ball, merely picking out an intermediate cause says nothing about intention.

The Illusion of Control

We can claim that we intended to think about bicycles, but to really be in control, we'd need to look at the source of this intention. Why did we decide to think about bicycles? Was it spontaneous? No control there. Was there a cause? If so, it's merely an intermediate step and we need to be looking at *its* cause. And around and around we go.

If we can't logically control spontaneous thoughts or thoughts with prior causes, what exactly are we left controlling? By what other possible way can a thought arrive in our conscious mind?

What becomes evident is there is no logical way to explain how we can originate any of our thoughts. But can that really be right? All our choices and actions stem from thought, thus if we don't control those, how are we in control of anything? That's inconceivable! But how many of us ever really examine the mechanics of thoughts for logical consistency? And we here are, with two of the prime elements of illusion.

Just like the visual field, feeling that we experience a certain phenomenon is not evidence that we do. Despite going about our day under the assumption that we're consciously controlling our own thoughts, logically speaking, it can't be. We're just not prone to consider the origin of every thought we have. But when we do, there is only one conclusion we can reach: control is perhaps the most fantastic illusion of all.

9 ~ The Evolution Cycle

The process by which modern organisms descended from our ancient ancestors is stunning. In a billion years, our ancestors have evolved from microorganisms into every form of life we know today.

What might that mean for the next billion years?

The short answer is we have no idea. Who could have predicted that humans, cats, dogs, bears, trees, plants, grass, insects, or any life form, could have evolved from bodies of water filled with microorganisms.

When you add the impact of technology, where future humans may be able to rewire themselves or reprogram their own DNA, it's clear that any predictions about what's possible are futile.

Yet there are some intriguing patterns that arise if you look far enough back in history. There are cycles that seem to keep repeating. Let's take a look through some of the basic stages.

The History of Life

Somewhere between 500 million and 1 billion years ago, multicellular complex life forms began to **crawl** around the ocean floors. To them, the floor was their entire universe, and crawling permitted new ways to explore.

Then, millions of years later, the ability to swim arose. The proto-amphibians were able to leave the ocean floor and **traverse** through the water, examining an entirely new environment. Their universe had suddenly expanded.

But these proto-amphibians could not leave the ocean. They could not breathe in what lay outside the waters. They may have been aware that something existed beyond the water, and some may have even momentarily left the ocean, but they were still limited.

Then something interesting happened. After a tremendously large number of mutations over several hundred million years, these life forms were able to **adapt**. For some lifeforms beneath the ocean floor, a new environment existed, open to exploration and wonder.

In time, amphibians began crawling on the land, repeating the process of investigation that their ancestors had done on the ocean floor millions of years prior. The mutating continued for several hundred million years, eventually producing humans.

Humans developed the ability to leave the floor of the earth and traverse through the air. But we cannot breathe in what lies outside the atmosphere. We are aware that something exists beyond the planet, some of us even having left it momentarily, but we are still limited.

And thus the Cycle Repeats: Crawl, Traverse, Adapt, Crawl, Traverse, Adapt…

If this pattern is able to continue, the logical conclusion is that humans will eventually adapt to space. We will then be able to live in a new environment, traversing through it with the same ease of early fish swimming in the oceans.

If such an adaption occurs and whatever species arises is able to reach the edges of the universe, what new environment might this future species peek in to?

10 ~ Communication

A seven year old boy was discovered in Russia who was unable to speak. His only mode of communication was chirping. There was nothing wrong with the boy's intellect. He was fully capable. This was a case of environmental nurturing.[1]

He had spent his entire life living in a room surrounded by cages of chirping birds. His mother refused to speak to him, only engaging with him enough to keep him alive.

To this boy, chirping was normal. He had no idea that he lacked any other communication abilities. For all we know, he was perfectly content living as a bird in a human body.

---

[1] Cockcroft, L. (n.d.). Russian 'bird-boy' discovered in aviary. Retrieved March 10, 2016, from www.telegraph.co.uk

As strange as this situation sounds, none of us are immune to such notions. Imagine that you had spent an entire lifetime never seeing, riding, or knowing that bicycles existed. You would not only lack the ability to ride a bike, you would be oblivious to the very idea. Yet you do know about bicycles, and thus you consider bike riding to be a normal activity. And therein lies the crux of the matter. What is normal?

Normality

The dictionary defines normal as "conforming to the standard". Yet standards are subjective. Every culture across the planet has a different view on what is normal. Even time plays a part in how we define normal. What is routine or fashionable today will no doubt seem old fashioned sometime in the future.

So if your abilities are based on what is normal, and based on what your environment has taught you is normal, then how are you any different than the boy who could only chirp? How can you be certain that your capabilities are not limited by a lack of experience?

What if there is a mode of communication far more effective than speaking, reading, and writing, that just eludes us all because nothing in our environment has made it apparent to us?

What if when you speak, your words sound as crude as chirping to a more advanced or future life form? Perhaps, just like the boy, you have abilities that remain hidden because you don't even know to look for them.

11 ~ Evolution of AI - Part 1

In less than a century, computer processing has evolved from solving basic math to running software capable of operating self-driving cars.

When you consider that we literally turn sand into microchips (silicon comes from sand), and these chips support technology used to advance nearly all facets of life, you cannot deny that we've come a long way with computing technology in a very short period of time.

Science fiction has raised our expectations a bit high in some areas. Humanoid robots have been a mainstay in futuristic movies and books for generations. But that shouldn't stop us from asking what is possible.

Is Artificial Intelligence (AI) Possible?

Can we artificially create consciousness? No one knows yet, though many feel strongly one way or the other. If artificial intelligence is possible, it would be on the basis that every life form we know of is made up of atoms. There are only 109 atoms that we've found so far that make up everything in the universe, including the human brain.

From an atomic perspective, we only need to know the specific arrangement of atoms to recreate the human brain. Yet we may not even need to arrange things at an atomic level.

What if you were to replace every neuron in your brain with a silicon wire capable of processing data in the exact same manner? Would your brain still work? Might it be more efficient?

From what we know of neurons, this idea isn't that far-fetched. The sole reason we don't consider using biological materials like neurons for computing is because neurons themselves are not great conductors. Silicon is much better for the use of processing information.

It is conceivable we could create higher functioning hardware than our biological brains, and who knows what that might mean.

Software

The problem is software. No matter how impressive the hardware, without software capable of emulating the manner that the brain processes information, we're not going to produce AI.

Many incredibly capable minds are working on solutions in an attempt to understand how the brain operates. There is progress being made. We're just much further ahead with regards to the physical parts of the brain than the software. But have patience. The human brain evolved over 4.6 billion years. The evolution of computing has only just begun.

Evolution of AI

All software is rooted in binary coding – 1's and 0's. With a long enough string of them, you can represent any amount of information.

Everything you know that is based on technology is binary. The software that runs the top chess playing programs, the IBM Watson computer from Jeopardy, the Mars Rover, and all the data going in and out of your computing devices – all of it is reducible to a string of 1's and 0's.

If there were a program written to bring AI consciousness, no matter how complex the software, it could be represented by a single string of binary code. If we refer to the total number of 1's and 0's in this code as X, the odds of randomly discovering this code are $1/2^X$.

(2^X = total number of possible combinations of X)

Since we can assume X would have to be extraordinarily large, we can also safely assume $1/2^X$ is ridiculously small.

For a program of size X to evolve randomly, the number of iterations required would have to vastly exceed 2^X. Given that we don't know X, we can't even guess at how long that might take.

Engineering

Advances in technology are not made randomly. The evolution of computing is entirely guided by human ingenuity, supported with specific planning. We are not blindly seeking a pattern for X. We are engineering a process whereby we build on what has worked in the past and develop strategies on how to increase functionality.

If AI develops consciousness, it will be the result of clear-cut intention. This is precisely why we've been able to go from giant room-sized computers doing simple math to hand held devices capable of answering your questions. The mechanism guiding this process is continuous feedback. We steadily progress by keeping what is beneficial and ignoring what isn't.

This process is exactly the same as biological evolution. I've merely inserted human engineers reacting to feedback on software in lieu of nature. The difference is that it took nature billions of years to produce something capable of doing even basic math. We've accomplished this and so much more in less than a century. If we're outpacing nature so staggeringly and nature produced us, what might we produce?

12 ~ Objective Reality

Though you may imagine your future and reminisce about your past, both only exist as thoughts in your mind. You are only able to affect the present moment. Yet is there even a present?

Consider that everything you perceive must travel through neurons to reach your brain. At light speed, the time it takes may seem insignificant, but the reality is that everything you sense occurred prior to your awareness of it.

It is therefore physically impossible to perceive anything the moment it happens. Even your perception of the present is a memory.

For practical purposes this doesn't matter, but from a philosophical standpoint, its raises some issues. If the past, future, and present all exist only as thoughts, what are we left with?

Objectivity

We're left with reality, right? An objective one to be precise. Regardless of what is perceived, there is an objective reality. But how can you be so certain?

If everything you know about reality is based on perception, how can it be objective? What is there about reality that isn't perceived? Even the idea of a reality outside of perception is still a perception.

The closest thing we have to an "objective reality" is an "agreed upon reality". We all agree the moon is there, whether any of us perceive it at any specific moment in time or not.

Yet there is nothing absolute about an agreed upon conclusion. Facts are not defined by consensus. Thus if you follow the logic, isn't it more sensible to conclude that "objective reality" is not a fact, it's merely a hypothesis?

13 ~ Depth of Knowledge

For centuries mental disorders such as schizophrenia and epilepsy were a total mystery. Witnessing someone experiencing the then unknown effects of these disorders led to lots of confusion.

People were not just perplexed, they were afraid, and assumptions were made. As a result, in a lot of cultures people with epilepsy or schizophrenia were shunned and sometimes even thrown in prison. It was believed to be a sign of attack by demons or witchcraft, an accusation that often lead to execution.

Perhaps worst among all the remedies was what occurred during medieval times. It was believed that evil spirits were trapped inside the head of one of these innocent victims. In extreme instances, the head was cut open and a portion of the brain was removed.

Knowledge

We're fortunate to live at a time when neural disorders are much better understood. We know things about the inner-workings of the brain that weren't even conceivable a few generations ago.

Children today know more about the human body (and the world around us) than anyone did a millennium ago. This is due to the considerable growth in scientific understanding over time.

There's still far to go. Science has barely begun to understand human consciousness. Yet many people today are just as willing to fill in the gaps of knowledge with assumptions about consciousness and human awareness.

Our history in dealing with mental disorders prior to better understanding the brain raises some captivating questions about our assumptions today.

What might we discover about consciousness in the future that seems unreachable today? What current actions do we take as a society that future generations might look back on with disgust due to our faulty assumptions? How confident should any of us be about our current views regarding the brain and mind? How far into the future must we project to reach a state when our current understanding is beneath that of the average child?

14 ~ Morality & Accountability

A man roams into a large city equipped with a knife and begins to attack anyone he sees, mutilating many and ultimately killing a pedestrian. We lock him up or put him to death, but we don't question his lack of morality.

Later we discover this man had developed a brain tumor. Until very recently he had exhibited no signs of aggressive behavior nor had he any prior history of criminal activity. He was a very fine and upstanding member of society whose personality completely changed due to pressure on his frontal lobe. As a result of the tumor, doctors conclude that he had no conscious control over his actions when he roamed into the city.

With this new knowledge, it is easy to accept that we must judge the morality of the situation differently. It is still equally regrettable, but ethically speaking, once we accept the actions were the result of the tumor and not the man's conscious intent, morally speaking, the situation is no different than if a bear had found its way into the city and done the same.

Accountability

It would be inhumane not to remove the tumor from this man, but that still leaves the question of justice.

If removing this tumor would fully restore his prior personality, would it be cruel to keep this person locked up given that he'd no longer pose a danger to society? Would it be sensible to significantly reduce sentencing, if not remove punishment entirely?

If we credit the intent, the choice, and the actions this man took entirely to the effects of the tumor, it would be nonsensical to hold him accountable in the same manner that we hold fully healthy humans accountable.

But what happens if we take this a step further?

Neurotransmitters

Imagine a future where a tendency for violent behavior is determined to be the result of defective neurons in the brain ~ neurons that we could fix.

Suppose it was possible to remove the tendency from any human, making it possible to alter the criminal population living in prisons so that they were no longer a danger to society.

Would it be cruel to keep them locked up? Could you readily dismiss accountability for their prior actions given that the criminal intent may have been hardwired into their brains rather than the result of conscious intent?

In such a scenario, is there any difference between the seemingly immoral acts resulting from a brain tumor versus defective neurons?

Possibilities

As unrealistic as this dilemma may seem, it is not outside the realm of possibility. Neuroscience has already found that many mental disorders are caused by defective neurotransmitters.

We hold someone with severe schizophrenia who commits a crime to an entirely different level of accountability than someone with no signs of mental disorders who commits the same crime. Thus, if we were to discover that any propensity for violent behavior is related to a physical mental disorder, this would change things considerably.

In the future, if such issues become curable, we'd have to look at how we deal with criminal behavior much differently.

This leads to the possibility that in the future we may be forced to consider whether criminal choice is the result of hard wiring mixed with circumstance. If so, how can anyone be held accountable? Perhaps more importantly, if we can demonstrably remove all defects related to criminal intent, is accountability even relevant?

15 ~ Sensory Deprivation

Bats have an amazing ability to use sound to understand their surroundings. They bounce sound waves off nearby objects and navigate by interpreting the data when it returns.

Humans do the same thing to some extent and most of us don't even realize it. The next time you look in your rear-view mirror, consider for a moment what is going on. Light waves bounce off the road and vehicles behind you, deflect off your mirror, and run straight into your retina. Your brain interprets the data and gives you a visual representation of what is behind you without the need to turn your head. It is an amazing process.

The Science of Senses

Scientifically speaking, to have a sense there needs to be a sensor. If these sensors stop working, we lose the ability to utilize that sense. But this is limited to the physical senses such as hearing and sight.

We are also loaded with a number of senses that are derived from the physical senses. For instance, our sense of equilibrium and balance is based on detecting changes in fluid located in our ear canals. We have a sense of thirst and hunger based on our body's ability to detect changes in glucose levels.

Some senses are based on an interpretation of sensory inputs, such as a sense of danger or intuition. These senses rely on our brain's subconscious recognition of prior patterns which then produce a particular set of feelings. When you walk through the woods and notice the birds have suddenly become quiet, you naturally become alert to this change. This illustrates a very primal sense of danger that has undoubtedly served humanity well.

A sense of danger or intuition even works when we aren't aware of the changes; such as when subtle patterns or oddities raise our level of alertness for reasons we can't explain. Our subconscious recognizes items that fall outside normal patterns, and raises our alertness even when we're not consciously aware the changes. You experience this when you get a bad feeling about someone based on their demeanor.

The way all our senses operate together is wildly amazing. Equally compelling is the notion that our entire reality is defined by the information our senses provide. Every memory we have is a compilation of sensory inputs all mixed together in some form or fashion.

Value of Sensors

Without sensors, we sense nothing. We would literally have no mechanism for senses, and thus no way to create new memories or even establish a reality.

If we remained physically alive but had no inputs to define reality, what would the condition of our mind be? Would reality even exist to us, or have any meaning?

16 ~ Renewable Energy

If a fully renewable energy source became available that was environmentally friendly and cost less than oil (and its by-products), what would this mean to you? How would society change?

In this hypothetical situation, assume something truly revolutionary. Your car runs for tens of thousands of miles with no energy costs, your utility bills at home became negligible, and energy costs to industry become insignificant.

This seems like bliss. Among the positives would be:

- **a replenished environment**
- **diminished consumer costs**
- **lower tangential costs (plane fares, food prices, etc.)**
- **reduced funding to militant oil-based nations**
- **less warfare over oil**

But there are also many things to consider that are not

so positive. The worldwide effect on unemployment could be catastrophic. Of the 500 largest companies in the world, 59 are oil companies – that's 11.8%!

You also need to consider all the tangential companies that are not considered as part of the "oil" industry, but entirely depend on them such as pipe and drill manufactures, gas stations, and oil transporters. This also affects attorneys, accountants, and lobbyists who work primarily with oil related clients. You are looking at a colossal number of people would potentially be out of work.

Though consumer costs might decline, the burden on governments to support those out of work would be like nothing any of us have experienced. This could easily mean the entire cost saving benefits are countered by massive new taxes.

Although you may have little sympathy for oil companies suddenly facing ruin, you might want to consider how many of these companies are a significant part of the average retirement plan.

If you thought you lost value in the last major downturn, just wait until 11.8% of the biggest companies in the world aren't just down, but gone. There are many things that can cause a panic, but oil companies disappearing from the stock market would likely make 1929 look rosy by comparison.

There would be massive unrest from those nations either currently supported primarily by oil or heavily based on oil exportation. Some of these countries might surprise you, such as Russia, Canada, and Norway.

Though the biggest benefit may be the environment, you'd have compare what the tradeoffs might be. It is not always obvious. Consider the following study by Matt Ridley on US energy requirements that outlines the comparative needs of oil versus alternative energies:

> [2]"To supply just the current 300 million inhabitants of the United States with their current power demand of roughly 10,000 watts each (2,400 calories per second) would require:"
>
> - Solar panels the size of Spain
> - Or Wind Farms the size of Kazakhstan
> - Or woodland the size of India and Pakistan
> - Or Hayfields for horses the size of Russia and Canada combined
> - Or hydroelectric dams with catchments larger than all the continents put together.
>
> "As it is, a clutch of coal and nuclear power stations and a handful of oil refineries and gas pipelines supply the 300 million Americans with nearly all their energy from an almost laughably small footprint." [2]

While we have obvious concerns, the alternatives may bring about as many glaring issues as they resolve. Are we in fact stuck until oil runs out? Can these issues be handled if the process is gradual, maybe over 20 to 30 years? Is it worth the risk to replace oil and let things work themselves out? What would you do if you happened to discover this perfect alternative fuel?

---

[2] Ridley, Matt. The Rational Optimist. New York: Harper Perennial, 2011. Print.

17 ~ The Past

Have you ever wished you could look into the past? It's theoretically possible. In fact, you're doing it right now.

The closest star you can see is the sun, which is just over 8 light minutes away from earth. When you see the sun, you are not seeing the present sun, you are seeing it as it was 8 minutes ago. The sun could disappear and you would have no way of knowing about it for 8 minutes.

Some of the stars you see in the night sky are over 100 light years away. When you view them, you are looking 100 years into the past.

The brightest star you can see is Alpha Centauri, located 4.3 light years away (what you see is actually a collection of three stars). The light reaching Alpha Centauri right now is light emitted 4.3 years ago. If some entity in that region is looking at earth using a ridiculously good telescope, it is seeing earth as it was 4.3 years ago.

If you could find a way to put a giant mirror into space

several light years away, you could theoretically watch your own history. The farther away you put it, the further back in time you could see. If it was 50 light years away, you'd be seeing earth 100 years into the past.

All the light you have ever reflected over the course of your entire lifetime is still traveling across the universe somewhere. It may not be easy to collect, but your past is theoretically obtainable.

What about Something Practical?

I once was at a high school baseball game where two fields sat opposite each other with concurrent games being played. I found it amusing how I could see the crack of the aluminum bat hitting the ball on the field in the distance a moment before I actually heard it. It was fascinating. And then it occurred to me – *I was hearing the past.* This is the same phenomenon you experience when you see the crack of lighting only to hear thunder a few moments later. You are hearing the past.

The reality is that everything you sense comes to you after it has occurred. As fast as light travels, it still requires time to reach your eyes. The amount of time is so small that you cannot perceive it. As a result, it is not physically possible to actually see the present. You are, in fact, currently seeing the past.

To a lesser extent, when you record video and replay it, you are seeing the past in a form of stored light. It is not as romantic as putting a giant mirror in deep space, but it operates on a similar basis.

You have a manner of seeing the past that was not available to anyone living more than 150 years ago (and realistically much more recent than that).

Depending on your age, it's possible there isn't any

video of you as a child. Some people have only a few photos and memories to explain what they were like. But at least these people have photos. So much of human history had nothing but their own minds to relive the past.

Do you consider yourself lucky? The ability to see the past though video would have been a dream to most humans in history. Yet most people don't think twice about carrying around a small video device in their pocket. How much do you value the ability to look into the past?

18 ~ A World Without Ego

Have you ever wondered why people are proud of their beliefs? Why would you have satisfaction for having an opinion? Everyone has opinions. The act of believing doesn't require any effort at all.

In fact, it's the opposite that is challenging. Battling your own ego take guts. No one likes to be wrong, so genuinely opening up to that possibility is the real test of courage.

It's perfectly natural to ignore things that don't jive with your already made up mind. This tendency is called confirmation bias. How often have you had an opinion, heard some good reasons that indicate you're probably wrong, and still thought to yourself, "I'm going to believe this anyway".

Strong beliefs are just opinions you refuse to reconsider. Sure, you have good reasons for your views. Everyone does. But you're human, so you are just as susceptible as anyone to cognitive biases, bad judgment, and overemphasizing personal experience. John Kenneth Galbraith said it best:

> *"Faced with the choice between changing one's mind and proving that there is no need to do so, almost everyone gets busy on the proof."*[3]

If you should be proud of anything, it's having the humility to admit that, even when you're most certain, you could still be wrong. Can you imagine a world with everyone being so humble?

The Role of Ego

This is a large part of what ego is all about – that sense of self-assurance that makes you reject the idea of possibly being wrong. It makes you prefer to be agreed with rather than be corrected. You ignore those who disagree with you on the matters that mean the most to you. Shouldn't it be the opposite?

Often we deride those with big egos, labeling them as arrogant, self-centered, and lacking humility. You know the type. Wouldn't the world be better off without big egos?

But hold on. Why do we even have an ego? Do you ever wonder why the human ego evolved?

It's possible that humanity depends on the ego to continually progress – at least the part defined by a strong self-assurance. The need for some people to willingly take excessive risks, even when it puts their lives are at stake, has been a huge benefit to society throughout history.

[3] Economics, Peace and Laughter (1971), p. 50

The Wright Brothers risked their lives to prove flight was possible and we all benefit from this in immeasurable ways. Had they died in their efforts, other brave, assured men and women would have filled their roles as pioneers of flight. We just needed enough people to take such risks.

The Human Race Benefits by Volume

We only need a very small segment of risk takers to succeed for civilization to reap massive rewards. It's not always evident because we don't write books about those who didn't prevail. Inspirational stories about history are deceptively selective in this regard.

I'm not denouncing risk. I wholly agree with Goethe who reminds us that boldness has genius, power and magic in it. But for every great success like the Wright Brothers, there are perhaps millions of colossal failures you've never heard about – all of whom may have shared the same attributes and took the same style of risks as the Wright Brothers…yet failed..

Progress depends on this. We need a lot of people willing to take risk in lieu of seemingly very poor odds. Humanity requires a ridiculously large number of failures to be assured of getting some big winners.

So how do we repeatedly get massive amounts of people to continuously push on despite such poor odds?

Ego. It's the perfect ingredient. Question a man's pride or rationale in the face of long odds and you'll typically find it only strengthens his resolve to prove you wrong.

To the extent that the ego goes hand-in-hand with self-assuredness, humanity needs it. We need big egos. A lot of them.

Not every person with a big ego is a jerk. That's not the point. The Wright Brothers may have been fine gentlemen. But they were supremely confident in their ideas before they knew for certain things would work out, and that's attributed to ego.

How might things be different if human history was defined by caution instead of a willingness to forge ahead into uncharted waters? Perhaps there would be a lot more humility to go around, but there would be considerably less ingenuity as well. Would you really rather live in a world without ego?

19 ~ Survival of the Mind

The well-known Theseus' paradox proposes the question: If you replace each part of a boat one by one until the entire boat has been replaced, is it the same boat?

As biology has progressed, similar notions have developed about the human body. Specifically – if you replaced all the cells in your body, one by one, are you still the same person?

Recent theories about technology lead to even more fascinating questions along this line. It is theoretically possible that, as science continues to uncover the inner workings of the brain, we may reach a point when it is possible to model a human brain using computers and conceivably transfer our brain/mind to a computer. Though at best this is purely speculative given how little we know about the brain and mind.

Possibilities

Put aside for a moment whether or not you think this is possible and consider the following scenario:

In a distant future, you face a health issue whereby you constantly get more and more tired, so much so that the doctors tell you that your body is shutting down. You are going to die. You are lucky enough to live in a time when there is a solution, one that requires a new operation.

The operation consists of uploading your entire mind, all of your thoughts, memories and emotions (your entire personality) to a computer for a number of hours. During this period, you are effectively dead.

However, a brain is regrown using your own cells, a cleaned up version that doesn't contain any of the cellular garbage causing the issue of tiredness. When this is complete, your entire mind is loaded back into this fresh brain inside your body.

From your perspective, the entire experience is akin to any operation involving general anesthesia. You fall into unconsciousness and awake in a recovery room, fully healed of your condition.

For you, nothing seems different other than no longer feeling exhausted. Your personality and memories remain fully intact, and to anyone that knows you, they are unaware you've even had this operation.

This Raises some Questions:

- Would you be willing to effectively die in this manner to extend your life?
- Would this new brain/body version of you still actually be you?

Many people find this idea objectionable. Some call it cheating death, while others object to it for being unnatural or sacrilegious. No matter how you view it, from your own perspective, how would this be any different from waking up after a good night's sleep?

20 ~ 3D Singularity

The continued advancement of 3D printers offers some compelling possibilities. If the printers advance to a stage that some have in mind, they could provide a technological singularity that would change the way we look at society.

Imagine having a printer in your home capable of printing any of the physical items you need. For some, this may seem far-fetched, but 3D printers are already capable of printing more than you may think.

3D printing is no longer limited to the production of plastic tools. Many surprising items can already be produced using 3D printers. Printers have been used to replicate bio-material such as organs, skin, kidneys, and even a replica of a beating human heart. It's theoretically possible to print new limbs in the foreseeable future. Imagine how much this would transform the medical industry.

Even food can be printed. As hard as that may be to

imagine, 3D printers have already begun printing breads, sugars, even hamburgers![4]

These applications will inevitably make it into the mainstream. So let's speculate for a moment about the limits of what may be theoretically possible, because that's where things start to get really fun (or scary, depending on your outlook).

The Atomic Level

If these printers are able to print at an atomic level, limitations such as the need for raw materials and waste disposal become obsolete. At the atomic level, printers could take sand molecules and convert them into a pair of new shoes.

At this point, we need to feed the printers the proper organic matter to make this happen. But not at the atomic level. If you haven't figured it out yet, the end result of this could be what is referred to in the Sci-Fi genre as a replicator.

Imagine for a moment if 3D printers are able to reach this potential and take any material and print out any other material. Physical materials could be found as easily as scooping up some dirt (or any other material), putting it into your replicator, and having it print whatever you ask. The only real limitation might be our imaginations. It's conceivable that we could even have these printers produce another printer.

---

[4] Tom Rawstorne for The Mail on Sunday. (2013). The future of cooking? now 3D printers can make food. March 10, 2016, from http://www.dailymail.co.uk/sciencetech/

Yet resources are not unlimited. Even dirt. But with an atomic printer capable of rearranging atoms, you don't need an unlimited supply. You don't even need a big supply. You just recycle any items you aren't using that particular day, and when you need them again, you print them out again.

Utopian or Dystopian?

What would it mean if atomic printers came to pass? Would you still need to work? Would you have any need for money? If no one had any need to buy food, water, shelter, health, toys, you name it…what would the world do with itself? Would it destroy civilization or be a renaissance?

21 ~ Evolution of AI - Part 2

When most people describe the inner working of the brain, they inevitably arrive at a portrayal that resembles some sort of computing process. As a result, those focused on the potential development of artificial intelligence approach the problem with software in mind.

Yet is writing code really the best we have to offer? Are we perhaps limited by this paradigm?

Models of the Brain

Conceptions of the brain and how it works have followed the best known processing and energy producing devices available at any given time. Prior to the digital age, the brain was thought to operate as some sort of advanced machinery. Before that, it was thought to be akin to a battery. In the early 20th Century, the operation of the brain was even described as a switchboard.

Given that we will continue to adapt our metaphors as

science progresses, we are as likely to be as laughably wrong with our current views of the brain as those from the past.

For starters, the brain is a wet organ. There is nothing about computers that is even remotely close to the material that is in our head. The brain also uses chemicals as part of its operation, something programming has no answer for.

There may be a mathematical limit to what we can understand. It is possible we may continue to arrive at better interpretations of our brain without ever finding a model we consider complete. So what might be the answer?

Paradigm Shift

No matter how much we examine every physical element that goes into the development of a movie theater, right down to the nuts and bolts of the projector or the polymer of the film, we won't find comedy, drama, or romance. These elements are not found in the parts. There is a deeper level of understanding required, a way of looking at the end result differently.

Perhaps we're not looking at the brain problem correctly. Maybe looking at the physical parts is the wrong focus.

Biology has taught us that profound complexity can evolve from simple elements. Maybe it's time to scrap the idea of trying to replicate a finished working model of the brain and look to our own evolution for answers.

Evolution of Self-Awareness

Self-awareness may best be described as the ability to

understand the difference between you and the rest of your surroundings. We cannot find this in our parts. The atoms that make up every known living thing are not self-aware.

Even simple, single-celled life forms are not self-aware by our definition. Yet somehow, along the evolutionary line, primitive life forms had to have evolved from not being self-aware to a more developed consciousness.

Thus, understanding how this happened may be the real secret to the development of AI. And there's hope, because from everything we know about biology, there is a very logical and straight-forward process that may be the answer to how self-awareness evolved.

The Process

For any living being to sustain itself, it needs to interact with its environment. For things like plants and trees, this interaction is merely the absorption of light, which could be considered almost mechanical in nature.

For creatures that can move within their own environments, the interaction is more complex. Even simple organisms like sponges developed special cells that respond to certain stimuli - moving towards those that indicated food. Still far from a conscious endeavor, this represents a big leap from photosynthesis.

Over hundreds of millions of years, small mutations combined with natural selection led to more complex variations of light sensing abilities in things like proteins. This much we know, as it is our best understanding of how eyes evolved.

The more sensory inputs an organism developed to source light (and to distinguish light from non-light) the better equipped it was to continually find energy and to survive.

With every additional sensory input, you can create a better model of reality. For instance, with 100 pixels, you are pretty limited to the image you can produce. But with 100,000 pixels, you can create an image that gives a fairly decent visual of most things.

Models that better simulate the real world give an organism better chances at survival, thus as mutations developed over millions of years, natural selection would gradually produce simple life forms with mild abilities to replicate visual representations of reality.

The more sophisticated these organisms became at creating models that reflected reality, the better they became at differentiating themselves in that model from the rest of their surroundings. Here you can see the origins of self-awareness.

Once an organism recognizes itself in a series of models, it's only a matter of time until it identifies the differences with respect to change - recognizing the contrast between what has occurred and what may occur. And thus we have the roots of conscious planning, something that would be described as intelligence.

Is it Possible?

We don't know nearly enough about the brain to say with confidence that this is how self-awareness developed, but given what we do know with certainty about human evolution, it is no giant leap to say that this is a reasonable consideration.

So what, then, does this say of AI? Perhaps looking at the parts instead of the process is the wrong paradigm. Maybe we should be attempting to develop simple entities designed to find their own energy.

We can create solar powered entities. We can program code to replicate itself (good old computer viruses). Perhaps we just need to program a very simple entity that relies on solar energy for survival and can reprogram itself, and then set it free. Maybe this simple nudge, combined with time, is all that is necessary to develop AI.

Of course, one key question still remains: why should we want to create this in the first place?

22 ~ Efficient Unemployment

One of the big fears of technological advancement is the displacement of workers. If humans create machines capable of replacing most jobs, a lot of people will end up out of work. What if there are no longer enough jobs to support society?

Yet history has shown that employment is not a zero sum game. Technology can displace a massive number of workers while also producing many new opportunities.

Consider that, just under 200 years ago, over 80% of the employable population held jobs in agriculture. Thanks to technology and a lot of human ingenuity, that number has been reduced to well under 5%.

The Value of Efficiency

This is a good thing, not because displacing workers is favorable, but because making any process more efficient is a win for society. It is because of this, that you can walk into a grocery market with a few bucks in hand and find more than enough options to feed yourself for the day. But we forget, because we're not after mere nourishment. That's beneath most of us. We buy items based on flavor, and thus, a few bucks doesn't cut it.

Yet consider what it would take for you to produce some of the meals you regularly eat on a farm of your own. How many hours (more likely days) would it take for you to produce even a poor version of eggs, bacon, toast, and orange juice?

Make no mistake, technology will replace jobs. This is something that has continually occurred for centuries, and history has proven that not only should you be happy about it, but that you generally overlook how grateful you ought to be.

Why? Because technology makes things more efficient, and that efficiency vastly improves the average quality of life for everyone, even those that lose jobs in the short term.

What if it's Different this Time?

As the saying goes, past performance is not necessarily indicative of future results. What if technology really does eliminate the need for enough jobs for everyone? Suppose we're all fighting for a much smaller portion of working hours. What then?

Perhaps we're not asking the right questions. If you knew that you'd earn a little less money in the future, but you'd only have to work 50% as much, would that necessarily be so problematic?

Stretch it out a little further. If you knew that you could maintain close to the same quality of life while having to work only 1 hour a week instead of 40, wouldn't you jump at the chance?

Maybe the right question should be what we're aiming for as a society.

Why is Employment even the Goal?

The folly is trying to measure everything by a static definition of what is "good". If your income drops 10% but everything you buy gets 20% cheaper, this is a good thing. But not if you judge this by income alone.

Until the early 1900s, the 8 hour workday was not the norm. The average workers put in 12-14 hour days to make ends meet, and often worked 6 or 7 days of the week. You're asked to do a lot less today just to be average, but you don't compare yourself to people in history, you compare to those around you, so these benefits are overlooked.

Objectives

Our standards change with the technology we build. Why is working an 8 hour/day job so vital? We're so obsessed with trying to ensure that everyone can find full employment that maybe we're shortchanging ourselves.

Perhaps what's really important in the big picture is time. We want as much time as possible to do the things we love doing. Why not make maximizing everyone's available free time the goal? But this would require embracing technology in lieu of potentially full time employment goals, something not everyone is ready to do. Are you?

23 ~ Legacy of Ideas

How much of your life is influenced by what others think? I'm not talking about social influence, I specifically mean the ideas created in other people's minds.

Look around your home. Your table, your chair, your bed, your electronics, your automobile, even your entire house, all of it was invented by someone other than you.

Nearly every physical item you use began as a thought in another person's mind. And you've never met any of these people. In most cases, these people are no longer living. Yet their ideas endure, and they significantly shape your life.

Consider the opposite. How many ideas that originated in your mind currently describe any of the physical items you interact with on a regular basis?

It's more difficult to think of items you use that aren't someone else's idea than those that are entirely your own. And that's OK. There's no harm in admitting we all benefit from society in some way. But wouldn't it be nice to know you're contributing to the mix?

If life has a purpose, might it be to add to the collection of practical ideas in some capacity, so that your thoughts will produce a legacy of their own long after you're gone?

24 ~ The Mosquito

The average lifespan of a mosquito is 10 days. Though if one lands on your arm, you have no qualms about ending that life instantly.

That isn't because you are evil. Who isn't willing to swat a pesky mosquito? It's because of the way you view the value of its life.

Emotional Range

By all accounts, we measure the importance of any life form by judging the range of emotional states it is capable of reaching – the greater the range, the more important the life form.

You might think this seems too simplistic, but consider why you care so little for the life of a bug. The mosquito has an extremely limited range (or total lack) of emotional capacity. It's likely not even aware of its own existence.

Move up the realm of life forms and you're a little less willing to causally kill. Though you accept that billions of pigs, chickens and cows are slaughtered on a regular basis out of necessity, you would have a much harder time ending their lives causally, and for good reason. These animals clearly can experience pain, an emotional state that we don't see in bugs.

Move even further up the chain and consider how you view the life of a dog. Not only are they our pets, but we view them as having a greater range of emotional states than cattle. They get excited, sad, and can even seem to express guilt. Though their lives are not deemed as important as human lives, casually taking the life of a dog is deemed a horrendous moral breakdown.

The Peak

Of all the known life forms, we are very lucky to be at the peak. We know of no other species that shares our wide range of emotional states. For this reason, we consider humans to be the most important beings on the planet.

But this is where the danger lies in judging the value of life on such a spectrum. Are we really the peak?

The Issue

What if life forms exist in this universe that are so far advanced from us that, by comparison, our range of emotional states are laughably insignificant. We could be mere bacteria relative to their superior state.

These life forms may have no desire to bring us harm, and may be supremely moral and empathetic beings. But if they share our values, they could justifiably view us the way we view bacteria. Our existence could be seen so trivially that removing us isn't even a question of morality, it's just inconsequential.

We may want to closely consider how casually we eliminate any life. One day we may discover that humanity is viewed as just another pesky mosquito living amongst the universe.

25 ~ Transhumanism

TRANS·HU·MAN·ISM (Tranz-Hyoo-Muh-Nizm)
/ **NOUN** / **THE BELIEF OR THEORY THAT THE HUMAN RACE CAN EVOLVE BEYOND ITS CURRENT PHYSICAL AND MENTAL LIMITATIONS, ESPECIALLY BY MEANS OF SCIENCE AND TECHNOLOGY.**

It sounds like science fiction, but many believe there is a real chance we will evolve with technology – giving ourselves cybernetic implants and robotic body parts allowing us to become bionic versions of ourselves. With the help of technology, we'd overcome many of our physical limitations.

Some people love this idea, but many find it horrifying and unnatural. Putting aside what may be possible, is the idea of improving ourselves significantly with technology really so bad?

Consider how common **glasses**, **contacts**, or even **hearing aids** are at present. No one would genuinely argue that these aids are unnatural. Yet even in this simple form, they are technological improvements to our physical abilities.

What about other advancements. Is a person with an **artificial limb** less human? Would it make any difference if these limbs were regrown from cells or built to offer more range and strength than our natural limbs?

What about **knee** and **hip replacements**. These clearly represent the blending of technology and humanity, and they are perfectly acceptable.

We may scoff at the idea of a future where we improve ourselves with computers, but who among us would refuse a **pacemaker** to extend our lives? We can argue that tweaking our bodies to live longer is unnatural, but would we turn down an **artificial heart** or **lung** if it would save our lives?

To someone 100 years ago, many of the technological improvements we have available today would seem like science fiction – as much as implanting chips in our heads feels that way to us now. Some believe that is where things are headed. If the process happens slowly, who knows what will be commonplace and acceptable in the future.

Most people don't consider the extent that technology is already a large part of our lives and bodies. Is improving upon this really so bad? Is this something to fear or embrace?

For Lots More Thought Provoking Stuff,
Visit my Website:
www.the-thought-spot.com